In-line Skating
CHECK IT OUT!

Kristin Eck

The Rosen Publishing Group's
PowerKids Press ™
New York

SAFETY GEAR, INCLUDING HELMETS, KNEE PADS, WRIST PADS, AND ELBOW PADS SHOULD BE WORN WHILE IN-LINE SKATING. DO NOT ATTEMPT TRICKS WITHOUT PROPER GEAR, INSTRUCTION, AND SUPERVISION.

For Mike

Published in 2001 by The Rosen Publishing Group, Inc.
29 East 21st Street, New York, NY 10010

First Edition

Book Design: Michael de Guzman
Layout: Michael J. Caroleo

Photo Credits: p. 5 © Rollerblade, Inc.; pp. 7, 19, 21 © Thaddeus Harden; pp. 9, 13, 15, 17 © Tony Donaldson; p. 11 © Karl Weatherly/Mountain Stock.

Eck, Kristin.
    In-line skating : check it out! / Kristin Eck.— 1st ed.
        p. cm.— (Reading power extreme sports)
    Includes index.
    ISBN 0-8239-5699-7
    1. In-line skating—Juvenile literature. [1. In-line skating.] I. Title. II. Series.

    GV859.73 .E34 2001
    796.21—dc21   00-038528

Manufactured in the United States of America

Contents

Here is an in-line skate. It has four wheels that are in a line.

5

An in-line skater needs to wear a helmet, wrist pads, elbow pads, and knee pads.

This in-line skater turns upside down. People in-line skate for fun.

9

This in-line skater moves her arms and legs. People in-line skate for exercise.

11

This in-line skater skates on a railing. People can in-line skate on curbs, railings, and steps. This is called street skating.

J. Ber___
16yrs ___'8" 150
Bouch___ville
QUE

13

A halfpipe is a ramp shaped like a big "U." People can in-line skate on ramps and halfpipes. This is called vert skating.

15

This in-line skater is
upside down in the
air. Some in-line skaters
do tricks in the air.

17

This girl is shopping for in-line skates. You can look for the skates you like best, too.

Grab a friend. Get ready
to roll!

Glossary

curbs (KERBZ) Concrete or stone edges on a street.

exercise (EK-sur-syze) Physical activity done to get or stay fit.

halfpipe (HAF-pyp) A ramp that is shaped like a big "U."

helmet (HEL-mit) What in-line skaters wear to keep their heads safe.

railing (RAYL-ing) A horizontal (side-to-side) bar supported by vertical (up-and-down) posts.

ramp (RAMP) A floor or walk that slopes or curves.

tricks (TRIHKS) Special, or difficult, moves or stunts.

wheels (WEELZ) Round objects that turn to make a skate, car, or machine move.

Here is another good book to read
about in-line skating:

The Fantastic Book of In-line Skating
by Aldie Chalmers
Millbrook Press (1997)

Check out this Web site to learn more
about in-line skating:

http://www.iisa.org

Index

Word Count: 138

Note to Librarians, Teachers, and Parents

If reading is a challenge, Reading Power is a solution! Reading Power is perfect for readers who want high-interest subject matter at an accessible reading level. These fact-filled, photo-illustrated books are designed for readers who want straightforward vocabulary, engaging topics, and a manageable reading experience. With clear picture/text correspondence, leveled Reading Power books put the reader in charge. Now readers have the power to get the information they want and the skills they need in a user-friendly format.